I'm Not Far Away

A Message of Love After Death

By Peggy Decker

Illustrated by Tarmigan Decker

I'm Not Far Away: A Message of Love After Death
Copyright © 2021

All rights reserved. No part of this publication, or the characters within it, may be reproduced or distributed in any form or by any means without prior written consent from the publisher.

For copyright permissions, school visits, and book readings/signings, email peggydeckerauthor@gmail.com

Written by Peggy Decker
Illustrated by Tarmigan Decker
Edited by Misty Black and Shannon Jade
Graphic design and formatting by Misty Black Media, LLC

Library of Congress Control Number: 2020923656

ISBN Paperback 978-1-7362098-0-6
ISBN Hardback 978-1-7362098-1-3

First Edition 2021

*I dedicate this book to you.
As you read it, may you find peace
and comfort with the loss of your
loved one until you meet again.*

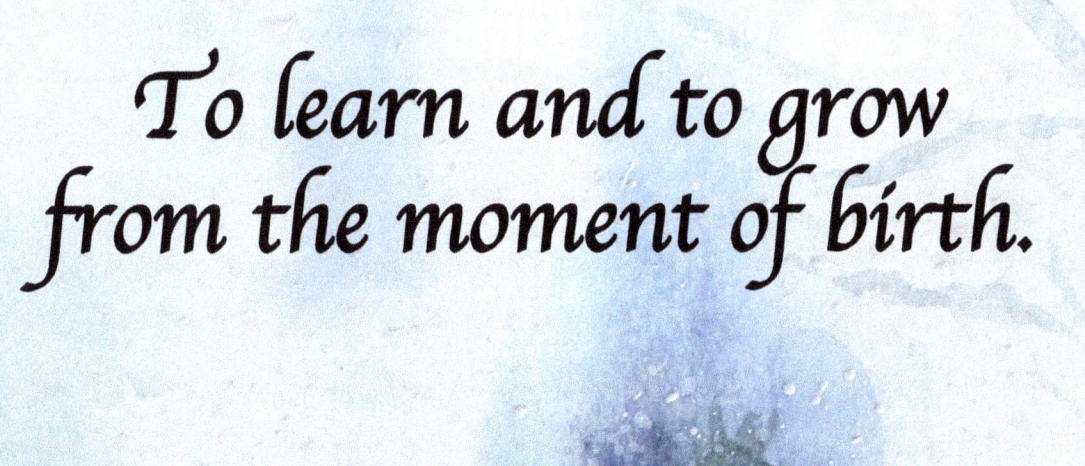

To learn and to grow
from the moment of birth.

Then, one at a time,
we each return home

to joyfully kneel
at the foot of His throne.

Our time together is precious and dear.
I cannot imagine me not being here.

But my turn has come.
Oh, how grand it will be
to meet all my loved ones.
They're waiting for me.

Please know that we both are right where we belong.

When you close your eyes,
let the memories flow.

Please don't cry for me.
Instead, let your light show.

This promise I make:
you'll remain in my heart.

A forever family, like from the start.

About the Author:
Peggy's biggest achievement is being a mother of four great sons and the grandmother of nine beautiful grandchildren. She and her husband are both retired. Spending time with family is her hobby. She also enjoys going to the mountains, and she loves the ocean.

About the Illustrator:
Tarmi is the mother of four wonderful little boys. She is a self-taught artist. Tarmi loves to renovate homes with her husband. She loves to cook and loves the outdoors.

www.ingramcontent.com/pod-product-compliance
Lightning Source LLC
Chambersburg PA
CBHW051305110526
44589CB00025B/2941